DHARAMSHALA DIARIES

STORIES FROM THE HIMALAYAN TOWN

DEEPAK RANA

To the pilgrims and the posers, the seekers and the sippers of chai—this book is for everyone who found their Dharamshala.

Contents

Preface

While there are countless tourist destinations around the world, Dharamshala doesn't like to compete with the rest of them. Instead, this multicultural town sitting in the lap of the Dhauladhars boasts the magic that's entirely its own.

The moment you enter Dharamshala, a cacophony of car horns greets you, followed by a constant stream of conversations flowing between pedestrians. Here, the world is a canvas painted with mystical shades, from the fluttering prayer flags to the flowing robes of monks, not to forget the postmodern aesthetics from Delhi and Punjab. The air itself is a curious blend of ancient and modern aromas—the lingering incense of Tibetan traditions mingling with the perhaps-less-ethereal scent of your perfume, dear reader.

Then, you turn your gaze north, and the mighty Dhauladhars rise before you. A sense of peace takes over, a feeling familiar to almost everyone who has visited here.

What, exactly, is this feeling? What makes this town special?

I've been pondering over these questions ever since I moved here, back in 2018. And while the answers remain unknown, the journey of seeking them has brought me a treasure trove of new questions—and some unexpected answers. To be honest, the essence of Dharamshala defies a neat explanation. It's an experience best captured in stories—stories meant to be absorbed, felt, and savoured. This, after all, is the heart of what I'm trying to do in this book.

Dharamshala is a small town, in case you haven't noticed. McLeod Ganj, the Tibetan settlement, is even tinier.

You'll find yourself bumping into the same friendly faces every day. As have I. This book is about all those people and their memories that have stayed with me in the last few years. You might spot yourself within these pages, or maybe not. Either way, if you ever find yourself strolling through the locales I've described in the following pages, who knows? We might just cross paths.

I

A High-Altitude Conspiracy

The year was 2012; I was in the town on a short trip.

A drunk Tibetan man, his laughter punctuated by hiccups, leaned against a tea shop near the McLeod Ganj main square. Across the narrow street was the Asian Plaza Hotel.

"Dharamkot," he mumbled, his eyes twinkling, "that's where you'll meet the craziest people, my friend."

I did not believe him, back then.

Now?

Well, let's just say you're about to find out.

৪৩

Dharamkot, like many mountain misadventures, plays a trick on first-time visitors. My first experience, in 2012, was no different. The walk uphill from McLeod Ganj, a good mile or so, led to a seemingly ordinary village. Standing outside the Himalaya Tea Shop, backpack heavy and shoulders slumped, I wondered what all the fuss was about. It felt *underwhelming*, a word that reasonably captured my initial disappointment. Tourist trap? Stewing on such suspicious thoughts, I turned back towards McLeod Ganj.

Dharamkot is not a place for tourists; it's meant for travellers. Or so the old cliché goes. But, like all clichés, this one endures because there is some truth to it. Dharamkot is meant for those who are willing to lend an ear to the whispers of the mountains and embrace the cool rush of a river instead of simply admiring it from the bank. If you do that, the place will open up to you. It is symbolic of the yoga and meditation that people practise in these parts. You may have all kinds of ideas but you only *know* what they truly mean once you experience them yourself.

Experience it yourself, I would say if you asked me about this place.

Dharamkot is a small village primarily inhabited by the Gaddi community. Traditionally, shepherds and gypsies, the Gaddis possess a rich history. Centuries ago, when foreign conquests became a constant threat in the plains of Punjab and Rajasthan, they were forced to make a difficult choice. Faced with the loss of their homeland and way of life, they sought refuge on the other side of these mountains: the Chamba district. There, hiding in the peaks, they believed invaders would have little interest.

As time passed and stable governments took hold, the invasions subsided. The Gaddis, while thankfully retaining their love for herding and the outdoors, gradually transitioned to more modern ways of life. They even built new houses in the foothills of the Dhauladhars, expanding their presence on this side of the mountain haven.

Calling Dharamkot a village takes some effort these days. Modern conveniences, once absent, are now readily available—everything you possibly need, including the less glamorous necessities. However, progress often comes at a price. The recent real estate boom feels like an encroachment on Dharamkot's idyllic charm. Will it succumb to the same fate as its downhill neighbour, Bhagsu, becoming entirely consumed by development? I can only hope not.

The village has a fascinating duality: upper and lower. Lower Dharamkot is a vibrant place, brimming with cafes and shops adorned with Hebrew script. You might even mistake it for an Israeli settlement (no, not that one!). This area is a popular destination for young Israeli travellers, many fresh off mandatory military services, seeking a carefree year of exploration.

"Go crazy in that year off" seems to be the unofficial motto, and Dharamkot, with its infectious vibe, caters perfectly to such ambitions. I once encountered a worried Jewish couple searching for their daughter, fearing she'd have found her true self and become a lost yogini. Luckily, their fears did not stand the test of evidence—she was simply enjoying the party scene in Kasol (near Kullu), her wanderlust eventually tamed by an empty wallet and a one-way ticket home.

The upper part of Dharamkot is relatively quiet. Or at least, it used to be. These days, its tranquillity fluctuates with the presence of young Indians flocking to the area. If they are from the South, you might be safe, but if they are from the North (like yours truly), then I would not say much, only that you should prepare yourself for an eventful evening.

Reaching Upper Dharamkot requires a dedicated walk on the cemented path next to the primary school. If that sounds confusing, you can ask anyone around the main square for Heena Cafe or Zostel—two landmarks from different eras that face each other in the upper part. Dotted amongst them are local houses, many offering homestay options ranging from budget-friendly to slightly more upscale, depending on your negotiation skills.

(Tip: If you're paying less than Rs 500, you're doing well.)

❧

This was where I first met Stefan, just a stone's throw from Zostel—a hundred steps up and then twenty or so to the right. Kush's house, that was what it was called. It must have been around midnight. I'd gone to bed early, like everybody else here. Then, a sudden cry pierced the stillness—not a gentle sob, but a loud, sharp cry.

"Someone better be dead," I said, but suddenly, a knot of worry formed in my stomach. You can never tell here. Mountain illnesses, when they do occur, often take a dire turn. Medical care is limited, and the general attitude towards emergencies seems somewhat... let's say relaxed. Everything else, however, is well-catered to: yoga, ayurveda, Tibetan remedies, and even the occasional black magic service.

Only in the morning did I find out that it was Stefan who had cried all night. It was a bit hard to believe—a blonde man in his forties, with broad shoulders and noticeably tanned hips. How did I know the details? Because he was brazenly sunbathing nude in the courtyard. It was a cultural shock, but I tried to keep the judgement to myself.

"I am Stefan," he waved.

"St-what?" I said. It usually happens with me when it comes to foreign names.

"Stefan."

"Stephen, right?"

"No. That's more English. I am German. Big difference."

Is there? As an Indian, I was not too sure about that. We like white people wherever they come from. *You are all Angrez to us.* I wanted to say this and more... Alas, I did not.

Despite our awkward first meeting, Stefan and I hit it off surprisingly well. He had his quirks, including a tendency towards Nazi sympathies, but if you could overlook some of these political views, he came across as a good guy. Also, he had a smile that never seemed to fade—whether he was puffing on a joint or reminiscing about a wild night of stargazing from his bed. That grin was practically glued to his face, day or night.

One of those days, I saw his smile turn into a frown.

"What are you watching?" he asked me as he arrived after a long walk in the evening. The sun had set and crickets had started chirping, and Stefan's smile had stayed where it was meant to.

"Nothing," I put my cell phone aside, trying to be polite. "Just a random video from Neil de Grasse Tyson. You know him?"

"Know him?" He put his hands on his head, almost laughing. "I hate him."

"What? Why would you hate a scientist?" I said. I don't know why I asked that question, but I did. In hindsight, it wasn't such a good idea.

"Let me tell you something," he paused to roll his joint, which took an eternity. I waited with all the patience in the world. "This guy..." he said and paused for another few minutes, "he is not a scientist."

"What? What do you mean? What is he, then?"

"An actor. That's what these guys do. They act. And he has been an actor since his college days. I have done a lot of research. A lot of—"

"Wait, wait... Do you really believe all those conspiracy theories?"

"I disagree."

"What do you mean?"

"They are not conspiracy theories."

I waited for him to continue.

"There is research—research that is not out there," he said, "kept away from the brainwashed public."

There was silence, a long and uncomfortable one. He smoked a few puffs; I stared at the valley and the changing colours of the sky behind it. It's one of my favourite things here: the colour of the sky at sunset.

"What about NASA? Do they not work then?" I finally broke the silence after a good few minutes had passed.

"They are a theatre company," he said annoyingly as if he was explaining an obvious thing to an idiot. Then he lit a cigarette. First of the evening. "All they do is, hire actors. A good way to get funding, you see?"

"Where do they go for space missions?"

"I don't know. Ask them. Maybe Australia or something."

"And they don't do anything? Nothing at all?"

"Nothing. Just acting."

"And all these satellites? Technology? GPS? Who is building these?"

"All this is just a lie. They are making all this up to prove to people like you that the earth is round."

"What? The earth is not round?"

"It is not. There is no evidence. I have done the research myself."

"Okay wait. I have heard these kinds of arguments before. But, tell me, if the earth were flat, wouldn't you be able to see Mt Everest from everywhere, say New York? Just take out a telescope and..."

"That won't happen. Because we haven't got such big telescopes."

"But we have those things. That's how we see the moon and the planets."

"You've been brainwashed to such an extent that you think the moon is real?" he said. The smile that had been there all along seemed to melt away, replaced by a deepening frown. "No surprise, you went to one of *those* universities."

I did not utter a word after that. It was frustrating. I was pretty sure that the local pigeons understood the concept of a globe better. In the meantime, a strong cup of coffee seemed necessary to combat the stupidity of the highest order. I gulped the coffee and went to sleep.

໙

The next morning, I went to Uncle's shop (right below Zostel where Uncle's son Kush now runs it after Uncle passed away in 2020) for chai. There, I met a young guy from Delhi. I shared the previous evening's story and he listened patiently. Then he said, "Very hard for anyone to see the reality because of these stupid chemicals."

"What?" I was not sure if we were talking about the same things.

He explained a few scientific theories, which I could not make sense of. "There is fluoride in your toothpaste," he concluded. "That's the real enemy. It does weird things to you, even closes your third eye."

"What?"

"I could not have seen those aliens in the concert if it wasn't for my third eye."

"What?"

"Dude, I have to go. You can learn plenty of such stuff on my Facebook page. Here is the name."

I checked it. Pretty much the same things he was discussing. The page had close to a million followers. I had lost the argument, statistically speaking. So, I accepted defeat and moved on... and I did not argue with a conspiracy theorist for at least a year.

II

The Girl with a Red Hat

When you live in the mountains, you don't plan your days as you normally would in a city. I, for one, have never complained about such a sedentary lifestyle. When city friends text me about my "schedule," I can't help but chuckle. It's hard to explain. Life exists in a perpetual state of "slow-motion" here, a welcome change from the urban rat race.

Sure, some of you might scoff at the inefficiency. Refilling a gas cylinder, for instance, can become a huge task, easily consuming half a day, if not more. But then again, on those rare occasions, you possess the singular purpose of "gas refill"—something to hold on to amidst the existential chaos. That's what gives meaning to life, isn't it?

On most occasions, though, there is hardly anything to do. The day leaves you confused with its endless possibilities.

It was one such morning, a lazy morning to be precise. Time seemed to slip through my fingers unnoticed, a common occurrence in Kush's place where I still occupied a room. Stepping out, I was greeted by the giant sun, a meeting that I often avoid. However, looming on the horizon, were the telltale signs of impending rain—dark monsoon clouds inching closer with each passing moment. Thank God for that!

It's hard to imagine India without the monsoon. Khushwant Singh once wrote, "To know India and her peoples, one has to know the monsoon." These southerly winds, on their annual pilgrimage to the Himalayas, bring heavy rainfall (and, yes, joy!) to most parts of the country. The season has remained a constant muse, inspiring countless works of art and cultural traditions.

I think of this beautiful verse by the classical Sanskrit poet Kalidasa:

> "The rain advances like a king
>   in awful majesty;
>   Hear, dearest, how this thunder rings
>   like a royal drum, and see
>   his lightning-banners wave; a cloud
>   for the elephant he rides.
>   and finds his welcome from the
>   crowd of lovers and brides."

Does this remind you of a Shah Rukh Khan song from the movie Dil To Pagal Hai? It's not a coincidence! Poets do that all the time.

Anyway, I may have got a bit sidetracked there (like, several times in this book, sorry!). Let's get back to that specific morning, shall we?

As I stood outside, rubbing the sleep from my eyes, Tuffy made his grand entrance. Tuffy? He is an infamous local dog, annoyingly named the "mad dog" by some. At this point, I must tell you that Dharamkot (in fact, most of Dharamshala) is as much a place for dogs as it is for humans. In this village, especially among tourists, there's an unspoken rule: you may curse a man, but God forbid you curse a dog. I had been duly warned, not once, not twice, but over and over again. Most of these furry residents are strays, forming their own little gangs as they roam the hills, seeking love and food. Needless to say, they're all rather lovable characters.

Tuffy is an exception. He is neither homeless nor particularly lovable, a rare breed in his own right. Infamous for his mischief, he's been labelled everything from a petty thief (he's quite fond of women's garments) to overly amorous, and sometimes simply "dog," intended as an insult (not sure if it is one). Tuffy, it seems, couldn't care less about the labels thrown his way, showing no hint of remorse when caught red-handed in his shameless thieveries.

That morning, he ran towards me with his usual enthusiasm, ready to shower me with licks and playful nips.

"Go away," I yelled. I wasn't in the mood.

To my utter shock, the scolding was met not with defiance, but with a surprising display of manners as he promptly took a few steps back and sat there, tail wagging. I couldn't believe my eyes—had Tuffy suddenly developed a sense of dignity?

"Let's just go for a walk," I started an inner monologue, something I do all the time. The monkey mind is rarely quiet, always seeking some kind of drama inside the head, both hilarious and somewhat concerning.

"I think it's a good idea," I responded.

As I prepared for the walk, I kept wondering whether Tuffy could indeed make for a pleasant company today. Was it too much to ask for? Before I could think about that, I had fallen for the trap. I looked straight into his eyes. Have you ever done that? There's something about locking eyes with a dog that makes it nearly impossible to decline their requests. The silent charm never fails to work. And so it happened to me.

"Come Tuffy," I said and he obliged. We both headed up, towards the Galu temple.

A few minutes later, I spotted someone I saw every day. It was a little girl, perhaps around 11 or 12 years old, diligently washing clothes by a *kulh*. Now, if you're not familiar with kulhs, let me tell you about them. Kulhs are small streams that flow through villages. It's a common sight in Kangra Valley. They snake through the village like friendly water highways, passing by every house and fulfilling daily needs.

As I exchanged smiles with the little girl, my gaze fell upon her peculiar accessory—a green Kinnauri hat. I knew that it did not belong to her, but to the yoga teacher who had rented a room in her house. The teacher often paraded around in eccentric attires. Why? There was some conjecture around that topic in the village. Some believed he was trying to impress white women; others thought he was hiding behind women to conceal his sexuality. While it's hard to point out the truth, what I do know is that he had chosen this career path to get out of India.

"A woman will come and take me with her," he had confessed once. And the influx of foreign visitors kept his hopes alive.

Continuing my stroll, I walked past the last house in upper Dharamkot and reached the Galu chowk. From there,

I followed a path (it was *less travelled by*, in Robert Frost's words) towards Naddi. This route, though shrouded in forest, is serene. With Tuffy by my side, behaving surprisingly well, we reached a meadow where I lay down on the grass. The colourful prayer flags were fluttering all around in the breeze.

Two hours slipped by as I sat there, doing nothing in particular. I didn't read my book, check my phone, or think of anything. Instead, I simply lay back on the grass and gazed at the flags. It's a practice I'd recommend to you as well—to let go of all burdens and do nothing. Isn't there a quiet joy in... existing?

After another hour or so, I resumed my walk, heading towards the Dharamkot main square. Today, the road wasn't as deserted as usual; it was bustling with Korean tourists, each with a yellow hat on their head. Of course, I could only guess their nationality, for I have never learnt Korean, Japanese or Chinese for that matter. But I can pick up certain differences. Korean feels like a conversation with a percussionist—a lot of consonants, a lot of emphasis. That's how I thought that they were from the land of BTS. (The other Koreans, from the north, would never have made it this far, would they?)

In all my observations, I still couldn't find an answer to the question: why was everyone wearing a hat today? Maybe I will never know.

Reaching the Himalaya Tea Shop, Tuffy bade me goodbye. The journey had come to its natural end, and so I did not try to force an extension. I sat inside the shop, ready to have a cup of chai, and... there was another *Hat-wearer*. She must have been around 30 and was wearing a red hat. I sat next to her table and stared at her sandwich.

"Tea is good here," she said, attempting to break the awkward silence. I was startled slightly, my gaze turning to her. She smiled; her brown eyes dilated in the afternoon sun.

"Oh! yes," I said. "I love it here."

"Alisha Rana," she said.

"Deepak Rana," I said.

"No way!" she exclaimed, a surprised change in her voice. "Rana meets Rana? That's got to be some coincidence in a small place like this, right?"

"I am not sure about that," I said, taking a long sip of the chai which had just arrived. "In Himachal, you meet Ranas in every nook and corner."

"So... you're from Himachal?"

"Yes," I said, pointing towards Kush's house in the upper part. "I live here only."

"That's such an Indian thing to say, no?" she teased and imitated my voice, "Here only."

"Actually," I chuckled, "that's also an Indian thing to say—No with a question mark. That's the case, no?"

"Guilty," she raised her hand.

"What about you?" I asked. "Where are you from?"

"Originally, a small town in Bihar," she revealed, "but Delhi's been my home for the last few years. Studying at JNU, actually."

"JNU, eh?" I raised an eyebrow. "Sounds like you might be a bit of a... I don't want to use that word."

"Communist?"

"I did not use that word," I grinned.

"You won't believe it," she said, returning my grin. "But let's not get into political debates on a beautiful day like this."

"Fair enough," I conceded. We settled into an easy conversation, swapping stories about our lives. I told her about growing up in a mountain village, the unsupervised play, the lack of seriousness in education, and much more. She, in turn, shared snippets of her life in Bihar. Security guards weren't optional; the risk of ransom kidnappings was a constant threat. She felt much safer in Delhi, which was news to me.

"I like JNU," she added to the last part of her biography. "Doing research and teaching undergraduate students, it's a good life."

"You don't look that old to be a teacher," I said.

"Really? How old do I look?" she asked, a mischievous glint in her eyes.

"Hardly above 22 or 23," I said, surprised by my dishonesty... or politeness. It's hard to tell the difference.

She threw her head back and laughed, and the sound echoed in the stillness of the little shop. "You're such a liar."

"That I am."

We continued chatting. Lost in the endless gossip, I somehow found myself staring down a political debate. How did that happen? I couldn't recall. I just remember that moment when she launched into a passionate tirade against communism.

"Look," she said, "This whole equality thing sounds great in theory... but in practice?"

"I know, right?" I said, unsure of what else to say.

"All these professors, they keep saying everything should be free, healthcare, education, blah-blah! It's like they've never heard of personal responsibility. It suffocates me."

"Yeah, it's a mess," I said. How many responsibilities did I have? I thought about that and felt miserable.

"You know," she interrupted, "I don't quite like when someone agrees with me this much."

"What's wrong with that?"

"I can't say," she admitted. There was a sense of vulnerability in her voice. "It's just naive, don't you think?"

"Maybe the world needs a little more naivete," I said.

She smiled. As the sun dipped behind the deodars, casting long shadows across the village, a comfortable silence settled between us.

"Well," she rose and picked up her bag, "as much as I'd love to stay and discuss these utopian societies, I will have to go. But I will be here tomorrow. See you, Mr Rana."

"Sure!"

The next afternoon, with boots laced and a small bag slung over my shoulder, I was about to walk down to the tea shop. And then... then I stopped. A picture flickered in my mind: Alisha, her smile, her brown eyes, reflecting the golden light of the setting sun.

Is it a good idea? I paused for a few moments.

We had a good time yesterday. Can I not leave it at that? Do we need to create the same stereotypical script for every male-female interaction? Sometimes I wish I could think a little less. But in that moment, the wheels of my mind kept turning, the same thought churning over and over. Maybe I didn't need to follow the script. Maybe some connections are different, like fireflies—beautiful bursts of light and that's it. They yearn not for our grasp, only for appreciation.

Did I make it to the tea shop? Let's not talk about that.

III

The Misunderstood Ghost

There might be religious, linguistic, cultural, class or caste divisions in this country, but...

(And there is a big BUT here.)

The whole thing changes when it comes to mystics, occultists, and practitioners of black magic—no one cares whether it's Hindu or Muslim, from this caste or that. Suddenly, the divide vanishes, and they find a common ground. Yes, people from one community may hesitate to fully embrace the beliefs or customs of the other, but those who appreciate the art of black magic carry no doubts about the power of dark forces, be it from any religion. Ghosts, in that regard, are truly secular creatures.

A couple of years ago, I discovered a thriving market for a Muslim occultist in a village just a few miles away from Dharamshala, catering to a predominantly Hindu clientele.

How did I get into all this, you might ask? Let me tell you about that.

Have you travelled from Dharamshala to McLeod Ganj, through the winding road of military cantonment? Doesn't it give you a sense of intrigue? It certainly does that to me. Soon after the small market of Forsyth Ganj, when the Church of St. John emerges, I get restless for some reason. There is something about its old stones, weathered and worn, its structure casting long, unsettling shadows. The air around it feels heavy, thick with deodar scents. It's different.

You may not agree with the above description. That's because you must have been there during the day. Sunshine tends to gloss over its creepy vibes. Then there are tourists, who constantly chatter and click selfies. None of it is there at night. That's when the hush falls over the scene. That's when the darkness looms and the whispers of history, the ghosts of the past reach out to talk to you.

To make matters more chilling, on either side of the church, you'll find a cemetery. Here, among the tombstones, one name stands out: George Davies. It is said that you don't forget his name once you've read it somewhere. So, good luck!

Wait...

What was I doing there at night?

Well, I had a bet with Ajaz, a Kashmiri friend, who is a firm believer in ghosts (among other things). The bet was that I had to visit the cemetery any time after 10 PM and it would lead to me getting choked in sleep at 3 AM in the night. Why 3 AM in particular? I don't know the reason but I assumed that the Hollywood horror movies had brainwashed his Kashmiri head.

"There will be a Christian ghost. So, he won't run away if you chant Hindu Gayatri Mantra or Islamic Dua," he had warned.

I went to the church late at night, around 11 PM. Stars peeked through the darkening sky. There was a complete silence; I could hear my own footsteps. Was someone following me? I had heard somewhere that you should never turn back in such haunted places. So, I kept my eyes glued forward and thought about all sorts of things to distract my mind.

"It's nonsense," I reminded myself. I didn't believe in ghosts, but I definitely feared them. That's the trouble. Because if I believed in their existence, I would know how to deal with them. I would be armed with holy water or some kind of prayer to fight the evil spirits. Unfortunately, that wasn't the case. I stood there in the darkness for some time, singing songs in my head to keep my fears at bay. How long had it been?

I checked my phone; it was midnight. What? Where did the time go? Regardless, I'd won the bet. End of story, right? Not quite.

A strange thing happened after a few days. I had gone to bed around the usual time. But then, in the middle of the night, I felt something inside the blanket. I jolted awake, a cool sensation crawling up my arms. Disoriented, I looked for my phone, the harsh bright light burning into my eyes. It was 3 AM. A coincidence?

My mind was not going to stop there—so I went ahead and checked the date. It was October 9. OH MY GOD! No way, it couldn't be a coincidence anymore. October 9 (1871) was the date of George Davies's death.

The weather didn't help either. The wind howled like a movie ghost, knocking at the windows. The trees, normally polite-looking, now resembled twisted claws reaching for the moonlit sky. Every creak of the house sounded like a scary cry, every rustle of leaves a whispered threat.

Feeling the butterflies, I ran towards the front door, flinging it open. There, bathed in the pale moonlight, stood a lone figure: a stray dog. That was a relief.

"A ghost will never hunt you in the presence of a dog," my grandmother used to say.

"Man's best friend," I thought, "Thank you for coming."

I spent the rest of the night outside. The dog—it was a dog and not some supernatural species, I hoped—kept me company. Sleep? No way, I was not going to get any. By dawn, I had promised myself that I wouldn't get into such misadventures again.

Later that day, I shared the details with Ajaz. He listened patiently, and then, he leaned in, his voice dropping to a low murmur. "It's clear. You'd either get a fortune," he said, and blinked a few times, "or disappear."

Those words confused me. What did he mean by DISAPPEAR?

"Anything can happen," he said and repeated, "anything."

Fearing the worst, Ajaz led me to do something that I could never have imagined. He took me to the occultist. Or *the good tantric*, to use his words.

ॐ

"He might be a Muslim but he is more popular among Hindus," Ajaz boasted as we drove to the village, the next morning. "That tells you something, right?"

"I don't know what to say," I said, rolling my eyes.

The house was located at the far end of the village. It stood there like an old man, burdened by the weight of years, the cracks on its walls mirroring his wrinkles. No one was there to be seen, no sounds spilling from the windows. The lone door, with ancient carvings on the frame, somehow managed to hold on to its rusted hinges. Ajaz and I exchanged a glance before we pushed through.

Only blackness greeted our eyes at first. Then slowly, as we took a few steps forward, shapes began to emerge from the void. A single candle, a lone warrior against the dark, flickered on a dusty table. "The good tantric," an old man with a beard that seemed to know no beginnings or ends, didn't bother with introductions.

"Don't worry, Deepak," he said, "he's not following you here."

Who is not following me? And how does he know my name? Did Ajaz tell him while setting up this meeting? I could feel the sweat in my palms. This was either the answer to my problems or...

The room was a sensory deprivation chamber. I was struggling to discern anything, so I couldn't tell if the words dripped from his tongue naturally, or if it was a practised performance. Were we being conned?

"I know, no one is following me," I said, trying to sound confident despite the tremor in my voice.

"But why were you following him?" the tantric countered, the light reflecting in his eyes.

Ajaz, in his ever-confusing style, joined in, "These things can happen."

"I know what can happen and what cannot," the tantric said, his voice dropping to a conspiratorial whisper, "but it wasn't wise of you to do that."

The urge to blurt out "Do what?" was a natural response, but I managed to keep it inside.

"You shouldn't go to such places," the tantric continued, his voice laced with a strange mixture of concern and annoyance. "They are meant for..."

"Ajaz asked me to go," I protested, pointing at the culprit.

"If he asked you to jump in a well, would you do it?" the tantric shot back.

Seriously? Rhetorical questions in this place?

"What are you saying?" Ajaz whispered, picking up on my muttered curses under my breath. "I cannot understand anything."

Taking a deep breath, I reached for my mask. Yes, those were the early days of the pandemic.

"Stop!" the tantric yelled, his voice laced with genuine fear. "Put that back on... Otherwise, the djinn will come out of your mouth. I've seen it. It's a Chinese djinn, sent to destroy the world."

I blinked, momentarily speechless. "A... djinn? From China? In my mask?"

"How can you not know?" He was surprisingly loud this time. "You live in Dharamshala, a town of all kinds of creatures. Don't you know what drove out the Dalai Lama? Djinns, of course. And now they're here, spreading sickness. Don't you read the news? People are dying, yes, they are dying. No one is going to survive this..."

"Not even you?" I managed to say, my voice barely above a whisper.

He leaned forward, his face uncomfortably close to mine.

"Don't worry about me," he said. "You worry about yourself, and that... thing... following you. Its name... we better not speak it aloud. Otherwise, it will cling on to you."

"What is this thing? What does it do?"

"So many things, there's a whole list. It drags you down, makes you feel like your insides are haunted by a shiver."

"Does it also jump from person to person?" Ajaz asked.

"Yes."

"Wait," I said to Ajaz, "doesn't it sound like a..."

"I don't know what you are talking about," he said.

"It's a djinn, you fools," the tantric said.

"From China, right?" I asked.

"Yes."

"The one in the news, right?"

"Yes."

"That's spreading everywhere, right?"

"You're really a fool. But yes, that's what it is."

As the tantric shared more details, we learnt that we weren't dealing with a Christian ghost—this one hailed from the land of Xi Jinping. Originating in China, it had taken on a multitude of forms, a shape-shifting djinn now gripped the world in fear. This is what happens when people move away from the one true God. The tantric ended the conversation with a long list of recommendations.

Drinks were prohibited. So, I got a beer bottle. Meat was prohibited too. And so, I ordered mutton Biryani. Then I drank and ate my way to sleep.

IV
It's a Lama Land!

The year was 2017. I used to live in Jaipur, a city with its own dusty allure. But, as it happens in life, I began to feel a little too comfortable. The magic that I had initially found there was slowly dissipating. A longing for something different, maybe a fresh perspective, had started growing in me. That's how, with a month carved out in my calendar, I set off for McLeod Ganj.

What did I do in McLeod Ganj?

I volunteered at LHA, an NGO supporting Tibetan refugees. I was supposed to teach English there. At that time, the office used to be in the middle of the market, close to the main square. Now, they have shifted below the Dalai Lama temple. It happened everywhere, after 2020. The pandemic redefined what we knew as the prime real estate.

LHA was a special place to be. You could learn English, French, German, Chinese, Tibetan and much more that went beyond linguistics—and they wouldn't charge a rupee. The idea was to help refugees by providing them with the skills to build a better future. Every day, from Monday to

Friday, I'd meet monks from different parts of the world. And I learnt to identify them by the colours of their robes.

Thai monks, for instance, wear a three-piece saffron wraparound with no pockets. Sri Lankan ones also wear a similar colour (there is a subtle difference in shade), but they can be easily distinguished from the Thais with just a glance, isn't it? An interesting case is Vietnam, where the colour depends on the Buddhist tradition followed by the monks. Mahayana monks favour grey or brown, while Theravada monks still go for saffron. Often, both these Vietnamese groups wear those pointy, bamboo hats, making them easy to identify. For me, it had become a funny guessing game which I played every day. The weekends were equally exciting. All of us, volunteers as well as monks, brought our brooms and cleaned the streets. I still remember every single day that I spent there.

☙

"All right," I announced one day, the whiteboard marker squeaking in protest, "Today's lesson: the present continuous tense!"

"What, what, what?" It was too long a sentence for them.

"You know what?" I said, "Forget the name for a moment. I will give you an example. Now, Tenzin, can you tell me what I'm doing right now?"

Tenzin, a young monk, shook his head thoughtfully. "You are confusing the students, Sir," he declared. A series of laughter, polite but amusing, erupted in the classroom.

"Not quite," I said, "but close. Dhonduk, your turn. What am I doing?"

Dhonduk, a Tibetan man with a perpetually confused expression, looked here and there. "You are... making a black snake on the board, Sir?"

Dhonduk was the kind of man who took things too literally. You tell him it's "raining cats and dogs," and he'd be looking for animals. He was a shopkeeper in the neighbourhood, so there was all practicality, no nonsense.

Almost everyone was laughing when Dhonduk mentioned the snake. Except for one nun in the corner. She never laughed; her face was a permanent resident of Serious Ganj; its population: only her.

"It's not a snake, Dhonduk," I continued, "It's a sentence. What is it?"

"Sentence."

"Mr Nguyen from Laos, perhaps you can help? What am I doing right now?"

Mr Nguyen was the oldest man in the room. He, too, used to be a monk, once upon a time. Then, he realised he was missing out on life, so he left the monkhood and decided to become a tourist guide. Hence, the English classes.

"You are... standing and talking very loud, Sir?" he said and repeated the last three words. "Very. Loud. Sir. Is that correct?"

"Well, yes, Mr Nguyen," I admitted. "I understand your point..."

Suddenly, a small voice came from the back. It was Karma, a teenage monk with a gap-toothed grin.

"Sir is... suffering?" he offered, tilting his head to the side. "Everyone is suffering."

The class erupted again. Even I couldn't help but laugh. "That is also true," I conceded. "But hopefully, with all your wisdom, our suffering will be over soon."

That's how each day brought some wisdom and a lot of laughter.

&

It was here that I met Lobsang, a young monk in his early thirties. He was a polite man—that's a given with the Tibetan monks, isn't it? Perhaps it's a sign of where they come from. Most of them have gone through perilous journeys at a tender age.

Lobsang, like many Tibetans you'd meet in the town, had arrived in India as a child via Nepal. The Dalai Lama is still a revered figure in Tibet, and many families ache for their children to meet the holy man and follow in his footsteps. So, with some hope and a lot of sorrow, they make a tough choice: they send their kids to Dharamshala. Lobsang's parents did the same.

The escape route adds more tension to the story. Families pay a hefty amount to an agent who then takes the migrants on a treacherous trek through the Himalayas, evading Chinese patrols. They travel at night and rest in the day, often hungry and exhausted, until they reach Nepal, and are finally declared refugees. That's where they get their yellow refugee cards and start a new chapter of their lives, either in Nepal or India.

Such is the level of hardships these Tibetans face, and yet they persevere.

Lobsang came through the same route and went on to pursue his studies here. He mastered his native Tibetan and secured a position as an examiner in the monastery. But he wasn't satisfied with this (not a great sign for a monk!). He wanted to learn English, a language that could help him learn more about the world.

Our paths crossed at LHA when Lobsang joined my English class. After the first class, he confessed that he wasn't exactly good at English compared to some of the other monks

"Can you teach me after the class?" he requested.

I readily agreed. He got a chance to learn English, and I, a glimpse into a monk's life. And so, it worked out well for both of us. We'd meet at Shangri-La (a cafe run by monks) and talk only in English, which meant that even simple conversations stretched into an hour-long affair.

Lobsang told me about his monastic routine. His days were filled with chanting, studying scriptures, circumambulating the Dalai Lama temple, and some office work, followed by chores in the monastery. Those of us who are a product of modernity might question such a lifestyle.

Where is the productivity in a monk's life, one might ask?

At the same time, the monk could also turn around and ask, "Where is life in your productive endeavours?"

It's a fair point. Long hours and bulging bank accounts have become our version of a 'meaningful life,' but it's not a bad idea to take a step back and reflect on our choices.

The monastic experience offers rich perspectives. Free from the constant barrage of distractions, a monk makes use of this quiet space for introspection. Here, amidst the chants and chores, lie the seeds of genuine connection—with oneself, with others, and perhaps even with the universe's grander questions. The feeling can be overwhelming for a new entrant. The world shrinks, then explodes in your chest. Tears flow out of your eyes, not from sadness, but from a strange sense of relief. The dam breaks and a lifetime of suppressed feelings floods out.

Lobsang's days revolved around the monastery and his room. The room was among the monks' quarters right below the Dalai Lama temple. It's one of my favourite spots in town. Instead of going to the temple (I mean, you can go but that's for another day...), take the path that curves around the temple to the right. The walk itself is a treat. The narrow path, the monks walking by, the prayer wheels, the glimpse of Dharamshala through the trees—it's a serene sight.

I went to visit Lobsang one day. He had invited me over for lunch. It was Monday, so the market was teeming with empty stalls. The usual chatter of bargains was missing from the streets. I walked with no particular hurry, arriving at Lobsang's place around noon.

"Hello," I said as soon as I caught sight of Lobsang.

His face broke into a wide grin.

"Deepak Sir!" he shouted. "Come in, come in... We were waiting for you."

"We?"

The room was a perfect illustration of minimalism. Three simple beds, a low table adorned with a threadbare sheet, and a bookshelf sagging under the weight of a few books with the Dalai Lama's face on them. That's it, nothing else. What the place lacked in luxury, it made up for in friendliness. Two other monks, Tenzin (with a strong, feminine voice) and Jigme, Lobsang's distant relative, greeted me with immense warmth.

"Lunch," Tenzin announced, gesturing towards the table. "We cooked it for you."

I was still thinking about his voice. Was he a monk or a nun? Perhaps it was an impolite question, so I decided to let it go and instead focused on the food. A steaming pot of momos sat alongside a bowl of thukpa (noodle soup), boiled rice and raw vegetables.

"Smile... before you eat," Jigme said, adding that it was an old saying. This philosophy, I had realised by then, extended beyond food. The monks cherished the simple things—the camaraderie, the smiles, the joy of sharing a meal.

As I devoured the momos, more stories came out of the hosts' mouths. Jigme had just arrived from Tibet (once again, the same method) and he did not know any language apart from Tibetan. He had learnt a few scattered English words, but each was followed by a lengthy explanation in Tibetan that went over my head. Tenzin was born in India, so he was fluent in both Hindi and English.

Inevitably, as in any conversation with a Tibetan, this one turned to the question of their return to Tibet. All three were optimistic. It might have been a distant hope, but hope is still a better companion than despair.

"I love the simplicity here," I said.

Lobsang, noticing my thoughtful expression, laughed. "Don't be fooled by the simplicity, Deepak Sir," he said. "These guys are crazy. They go to the waterfall and splash water everywhere."

"Do you swim in these robes?" I was curious.

He paused, then added, "We will scare everyone if we swim naked."

We all laughed like little kids. The simple joy of being in the moment, not thinking ahead or about the past, is something else. It was a perfect life, I thought after I took their leave. Should I consider monkhood?

I got my answers soon when Lobsang told me he would be leaving the town. The monastic life, while offering spiritual solace, couldn't fully meet his financial needs. Money matters, even to a monk.

Where was he going?

"Delhi," he said. "I will join some monks there for a job."

It was our last meeting. We spoke very little that day.

"Please take this for English classes," Lobsang pressed a small sum into my hand. I didn't know what to say.

"I can't take this," I mumbled, pushing the money back towards him. His hand remained firm, and so with a sigh of awkwardness, I accepted some of it as a token of respect.

Four years have passed since then. Lobsang has now moved to Arunachal Pradesh and started a garment business. Occasionally, he sends me a letter, wishing me good luck. This is the kind of wealth you cannot acquire anywhere else.

V

The Old Man and the Mountain

"Where are you from?" I asked William. It's the first question I ask everyone I meet (which doesn't always go well). People, these days, find it offensive when you enquire them about their origin.

"Are you going to judge me based on that?" they say grumpily.

William was not offended. He answered it with great enthusiasm as he did with most questions that came his way.

"Well," he said and looked away, "let's just say, I am from a place where you could spit from England and it would land in Wales."

"But," I said, laughing, "the question is, would you?"

"Look," he said, "at my age, you only talk about what has happened, not what can happen..."

We shared a laugh, and then, we let the silence stretch on its own. We stood there, close to the upper part of Bhagsu, gazing at the mountains, and at each other after hearing a distant birdcall. That's the thing about men meeting outdoors—we have this rule, to soak in the world without uttering too many words.

ॐ

William had come to Dharamshala after thirty-five years. Yes, thirty-five! The last time he was here, he was in his early twenties and the world used to be a lot different.

"So much has changed," he said, pretty much every day of his stay.

Many use this expression while comparing their memories with present-day Dharamshala, but in William's case, you could see the exasperation and nostalgia.

Back in the day, William told me, the Dalai Lama would stroll down the street like any other lama. The Americans hadn't given him the rockstar status yet. So, when he preached his ideas on peace, it fell on mostly deaf ears. Some locals even whispered that there was something nasty about him fleeing his homeland. Conspiracy theories were as common then as they are in Stefan's era. Apparently, the Dalai Lama used to hold exorcism competitions in Tibet. One night, he accidentally summoned ancient Chinese spirits who then, in an unexpected turn of events, made the living bloodthirsty. This led to what we now call the Cultural Revolution.

To be fair, the good old days weren't all that bad.

First of all, tourists were a rare sight (that's when you like them the most!). Secondly, 'progress' hadn't quite rolled into town yet. So, clean air and quiet streets were readily available to the residents. Shops were few and far between, with only Mcllo restaurant and the Parsi grocery shop next door as key landmarks. Bhagsu was still a quiet village, oblivious to its future as a bustling tourist hub with Punjabi music spilling from every corner. Dharamkot was a hidden gem, occasionally stumbled upon by a lost traveller seeking a simple homestay or even a night in a cowshed. So much has changed, indeed...

Such is the weight of old age: watching the world transform into a place you barely recognise. That's why, when William referred to himself as 'old man,' I knew what he meant.

The 'old man' defied his age with his enthusiastic routine. Up with the sunrise for a walk, followed by yoga in the forest, meditation at Tushita, breakfast with a local family, and to top it all—lively conversations. Well, lively except for one minor detail... he was a flatulence factory. He'd rip one without a care. We could be having a normal chit-chat, then BOOM! No regrets at all. And his farts weren't just bad, they were horrendous. Not that any fart is ever good, but his were from some other marshy planet. Was the price worth paying, even for his delightful company? I kept wondering.

ॐ

Every evening, we would sit by the fireside and discuss everything under the sun, metaphorically speaking. There was a group of Spanish musicians that added another dimension to our conversations. They would sing and tell stories of their travels. In between, we got William's comments. And while the stories went on, we would also bake potatoes or capsicum in the fire. Surprisingly, it tasted nice. Maybe it was less about the food and more about the company.

"There is something ancient about fire," William would say. "You sit next to it and you can share things you would not share otherwise."

"It saves from the cold as well," I would add. "Let's not forget that."

We used to bring logs and twigs and a bunch of pine cones for the evening fire. One day, when it was my turn, I got completely exhausted and lay next to the fire as William began to stoke it. Then, with the flames dancing and climbing, he began to praise them in his usual style. Behind me sat Amaia, the only woman in the group. Three Spanish guys, two holding guitars and the third with only his throat for an instrument, had just finished their song.

"So, Amaia," William said once the performance was over, "tell us about this wonderful Basque Country of yours."

"Please do that," I added. "I know nothing about it."

Amaia leaned forward and smiled, her grey eyes turning red with fiery reflection.

"It's a place unlike any other," she said. "You know, we Basques are the descendants of a lost tribe? Our language, Euskara, it came before Latin or Greek."

That sounded exciting. Did they really speak a prehistoric language? Lost tribe? I was getting more and more interested. William, on the other hand, showed no such enthusiasm. He took a thoughtful sip from his cup of tea.

"Amaia," he said, "if Euskara is truly that old, wouldn't there be some written records?"

Amaia paused for a moment, the fiery reflection suddenly seeming less playful and more intense. "Well, you see," she began, a touch of defensiveness getting into her voice, "most of our history was passed down orally, through songs and stories. The harsh environment wasn't exactly helpful."

"It is pretty much the same here," I backed her point. "The written word can't be the only measure to judge a culture."

"Exactly," she appeared more confident this time. "I know the English people don't like it. After all, they have a lot to hide in these matters."

"Excuse me?" William chuckled, and then he farted.

"I smell..." Amaia stopped herself, out of politeness.

"It's the smell of English loot," I wasn't *that* polite.

"I don't know what you folks are talking about," William chuckled. "What loot? Didn't we bring civilisation here?"

"Yeah, yeah, yeah," we all laughed.

"At least give us some credit for cricket," he said and took the last sip, "or this... tea."

"Sure," I said, "tea wouldn't have reached here from China. Thank God, you guys did."

"Let's hear more from Amaia," William said, sheepishly, while we all relished the moment of leg-pulling.

"Amaia?" he pleaded.

Amaia wasn't going to let go of her newfound audience. Who could resist such an enthusiastic bunch, anyway? So, she continued to educate us on the Basque Country's rich history: their fight for self-governance, their seafaring prowess, and of course, the long history of their language. We learned about Euskara's complex verb conjugations and its defiance against assimilation. It was a great history lesson, except that we knew that the facts had got a little twisted along the way.

William was a happy man—that's what everyone said about him. But occasionally, he was a sad man too. Sadness caught hold of him every time he thought about his life back in England. Was he running away from his problems? He told me about it during the last few days of his stay.

Life was tough. After a bitter divorce, most of his savings were gone, and soon, he found himself without a home. His daughters lived in London, and even though he visited them from time to time, he couldn't stay for long. This is one of the things I don't quite understand about Western culture. Why can't people keep their parents, especially when they are old and have nowhere else to go? Is it really worth it, to put individual pursuits over family tragedies? I don't know. Maybe these questions get caught in the current between Eastern thought and Western logic.

"So where are you going to stay when you go back?" I asked the old man.

"Just like here. I would camp near a mountain. That's always been my home: the mountain."

It was heartbreaking for me. Why didn't he talk to his daughters? Maybe they could find a way?

Yet, I stayed quiet. He was going to leave the next day, so it was a time for shedding burdens, not adding more.

"I will say goodbye in the morning," he said.

"Promise?" I asked.

"Obviously," he laughed.

Except... that he did not. In the morning, we discovered that he had left before any of us got up. He was going to trek towards Chamba. Through which route? Nobody knew. I felt a bit sad about the whole thing but I was beginning to understand the old man a little better.

VI
When a Dhaba Don Fell in Love

Do you live in Dharamshala? If so, then you might have heard about Charan Khad. No? Let me be your guide, then.

Take the main road out of the town, the one that goes to Palampur. From the police station, take a slight left, and a few hundred metres in, there will be a sharp bend. Keep going for around a couple of hundred metres and there will be a bridge over a non-existent stream. That's Charan Khad.

What's special about it? Nothing, in particular. Just that the protagonist of our story happened to work there.

৵

Vicky ran a dhaba which was on the left side of the bridge (if you're going towards Palampur). It was a small shack, built into the river bank in such a way that it seemed partially swallowed by the earth. I was there on the opening day. No, there weren't any ceremonies going on; I only happened to be walking by when a brawl caught my attention.

As it usually happens in India, a curious crowd had already gathered there. Men and women, old and young—everyone was drawn to the scene. We do have an obsession with roadside drama, don't we? And a good brawl is definitely among the top contenders. I craned my neck, looking for answers, and blurted out a question to the nearest onlookers, "What's going on here?"

An old lady explained the situation. That morning, the shop owner had shown up drunk and yelled at Vicky, saying he wasn't paying rent. A couple of his drunk buddies had also joined in the shouting match. That was what the conflict was about. Vicky, a seasoned veteran of such scenarios, knew what he had to do. He grabbed his favourite stick from the shop and gave those guys a good whack.

We all got a little excited when the violence began.

The drunks cried out—and Vicky kept whacking. That was my first impression of him: an angry young man from the old Bollywood movies, fighting the baddies with an ancient weapon.

৪০

Summer had arrived and I had moved to the lower parts of Dharamshala.

For some reason, my stomach has always craved adventures (and they have gone horribly wrong), especially at lunchtime.That's when I eat the most, and roaming the streets to find a new place to eat becomes my motivation. So, I explored most restaurants and dhabas that were around. Not Vicky's dhaba. The memory of that day did not allow me to visit for some time. Then one day, leaving the hesitation behind, I decided to go.

"Why don't you sit outside? It's nice sunshine," he said.

"As you say," I did not want to disagree. Thinking of the first day, I peered into the dhaba from outside. Damn! That stick was still there.

"What will you have?" his voice interrupted my fearful thoughts.

"What do you suggest?"

"I have rice and chicken curry."

"I would love that."

Surprisingly, Vicky was a nice guy. I visited the dhaba quite a few times in the coming days and weeks—turned out, the guy could do some chatting (apart from whacking!). The menu choices, though, were a bit limited. Daal and rice for fifty rupees, or chicken curry and rice for seventy. Still, not a bad deal, considering the chicken curry used to come with, well, two actual pieces of chicken. And if you asked for more, he would pour more gravy.

Vicky had lived an interesting life. When he was a teenager, he left his house and started working in a dhaba. There he would clean utensils. But the ambitious teenager wasn't going to stop at cleaning. Soon, he moved towards the kitchen and started cooking too. At first, it was just daal-chawal or roti-sabzi, but then he learnt to cook burgers, sandwiches, chowmein, momos, and more. Life was a buffet of possibilities—until, like an unexpected stone in his daal, a local girl showed up and that's it... It was love at first sight.

Vicky falling for her was expected. What was not expected, however, was that the girl too would fall for him. That's how Vicky saw it. In his words, life had taken a sharp turn, just like the one close to his dhaba. What he might have missed was that there was a social minefield on that road. The two of them belonged to different castes (not just different but significantly distant in terms of rankings). How does that matter? Well, what happened next will answer that question.

When the girl's family discovered their inter-caste affair, things went south quite quickly. A bunch of goons, led by her disapproving brother, attacked Vicky like a flock of angry pigeons protecting their nest. That's how men, at least in our society, see women in their families. The goons, believing in the same philosophy, gave Vicky a good beating.

The injured lover spent the next few weeks on the second floor of the local hospital. From there, he could see his lover's house. The story didn't end there, though. Our lovebirds had grown up in the 90s and they always had a backup idea when it came to these matters: elopement. One fine morning, they hopped on the first bus to Pathankot, and then... disappeared in a train. Nobody knew about their final destination.

For a while, the two were the talk of the town, beginning to resemble a local legend. The police were also looking for them. Where were they? In truth, as Vicky told me, they'd gone all the way to Delhi, got married, and started a new life there. Things were settling, a fragile peace holding... until a phone call arrived. A voice crackled on the line, delivering a message that would add another twist to the story. The girl's father had died.

Of course, it was a prank. A classic Indian tactic to bring the eloped lovers back home. Once the wife reached her parents' place, the family did enough emotional blackmailing to ensure that she would not go back to Vicky. But this time, things were different. Marriage had changed her. She could fight for herself. Besides, Vicky, the angry young man, had followed her to Dharamshala.

What could the parents do now?

Not much. There were a few tantrums (mother fasted for three nights, father stopped speaking), but in the end, they swallowed their pride and gave a nod. To follow societal norms, a repeat performance of the marriage ceremony was conducted. The couple settled into a small house in lower Dharamshala, but the differences remained between them and the family. Vicky, while tending the dhaba, would occasionally catch a glimpse of his in-laws passing by. Their averted gazes told another story. They felt ashamed; they still do, it seems. Vicky, on the other hand, can't help but steal a glance, especially when his sister-in-law walks by.

The dhaba is closed now, but for Vicky life keeps humming. An auto-rickshaw has become his new companion. Every morning, the two go from one part of the town to another, weaving through the streets, delivering fresh vegetables. Despite the hustle, life with his wife and son brings him joy. At the same time, a flicker of something unresolved remains. Whenever he catches a glimpse of his in-laws, he can't seem to look away. Perhaps the bridge is yet to be fully crossed.

VII

Life of a Modern-day Raja

When you think of Dharamshala, you think of the lush green Dhauladhars. These towering giants peek through a veil of white clouds, promising a breathtaking view whenever the wind blows and the veil lifts. That's not the case when you turn south, towards the lower parts of Kangra Valley. The hills shrink, the air turns warm, and the land bakes in the sun, painting the grass dusty brown. Somewhere in those parts lies the town of Guler.

Guler might not be the name you hear often, but it has a rich history—it's the birthplace of Kangra paintings. Let's rewind a few hundred years.

Guler wasn't the quiet town it is today. Back then, it was a cultural centre, brimming with legendary painters, the likes of Nainsukh, who invented a whole new style of Pahari miniature painting. These paintings were crafted using natural pigments with fine brushes on meticulously prepared surfaces of handmade paper or cloth. It was an expression of Pahari life on paper, capturing everything from love stories whispered under moonlight to epic battles fought by fierce warriors. Some historians even suggest that Guler, with its talented artists and bustling workshops, rivalled the grandeur of its neighbour, Kangra.

Now, Guler has been reduced to a sad, old town. As you look around, you do feel an air of ancient culture living well past its prime. The sight here, I must confess, carries some visual distress. When you get off at Guler railway station (it's on the Pathankot-Palampur toy train line), you will find plenty of buffaloes and cows roaming around in muddy paths. It's far removed from the usual tourist hotspots. Maybe you'd like it for that reason; it has that rustic appeal of the old India. Want more reasons? All right. Here, atop one of the small hills, lies the royal haveli.

One winter, a curious invitation landed in my lap. My old college friend, Narendra Rana, and his family were planning a visit to Guler's haveli, and I was included. The Senior Rana and I have been an unlikely pair. Decades separated our college days—he was a veteran of the 90s, I from 2011. That's probably the only thing I cherish about my engineering education. The alumni members keep running into each other, and helping each other, if required.

Reaching Guler can be a journey in itself. For us, it began with a drive from Dharamshala, going through Gaggal before reaching Nagrota Surian. You can also catch a bus to Nagrota Surian, if that works. From there, Guler is about fifteen kilometres away. The other way, as I have mentioned, is to catch the toy train from Pathankot or Palampur or any station in between these two.

(Note: Take the toy train at your own risk.)

As romantic as it sounds, the toy train journey contains every possibility to disappoint you. If you expect speed, don't bother. If you are obsessed with punctuality, forget it. If you seek certainties, well, there is no such thing here. Usually, you'll find one or two trains a day, and their schedules are, let's just say they follow the Indian Standard Time.

I have made that mistake a few times. Once, the train sputtered to a halt, its battery gone dead. We all got out and waited on the platform as the spare battery came to our rescue a few hours later. Then, one time, I had to catch a train in Pathankot and the toy train moved so slowly that it took almost seven hours from Kangra to Pathankot. I did not even make the entire journey and got off at an earlier station and hired a taxi from there. So, that's the risk! But... it's good fun if you like slow-moving trains. The ones where you can get off and get in as they move.

So, train? No, thank you. That's what we told ourselves that day as we steered towards Nagrota Surian. Did we reach on time? Not really, because, we were lured by the Masrur temple, which wasn't too far from our destination.

Masrur. The name makes you wonder. How did an Arabic word find itself in a Hindu temple? That remains a mystery. But let's put these linguistic concerns aside and talk about the artistic brilliance of the place.

This 8th-century marvel is a complex of rock-cut temples carved directly from a monolithic cliff. The most fascinating part? The entire structure mirrors the peaks of the majestic Dhauladhars that stand opposite them.

Like most tourists anywhere, we couldn't resist the obligatory photo op at Masrur. Pahari history whispered its secrets at every step, but deciphering them wasn't on our itinerary. Besides, in typical Indian temple fashion, an enthusiastic line for the 'darshan' (holy viewing) had made its way around the courtyard, filled with devotees more interested in blessings than backstories. We followed the norm and then we were back on the road.

We were supposed to meet Raghav Guleria, a descendant of the Guler royal family. The Senior Rana had schooled me on the royal man's life. Unlike his ancestors, Raghav's life unfolded in a different India. He dedicated himself to the field of education after university. Now, he is the chief correspondent for The Tribune in Dharamshala. Yet, a powerful pull draws him back to Guler and his ancestral haveli. While some might find this dedication excessive, Raghav is a man consumed by a singular passion: restoring his family's legacy.

As we got closer, the place appeared farther—something that happens in every trip. The haveli is in Haripur, about five kilometres from Guler town. The road from Nagrota Surian might be smoother, but the one we chose held a rugged temperament. This road, full of mud and stones, snaked through the villages, weaving between two gurgling streams. During the monsoon, these streams transform into formidable barriers, temporarily cutting off access. Finally, after our mini-expedition, we reached the base of a hill. There, a solitary board stood guard, saying: "Guler Fort."

The drive to the top of the hill was probably the hardest. There were sharp and steep turns. The entire path felt lonely, as if no one had been there for a long time. Then, just when I thought I was about to give up, we were there—at the haveli. All thoughts of a bumpy ride vanished, replaced by a tingling anticipation. It was time to see the restoration efforts of our host.

Raghav Guleria greeted us. Where was the crown, I almost blurted out. Here was a man whose ancestors led a royal life, shared the stage with the British elites, and now... well, now he was wearing a pair of jeans and meeting a nobody like myself. That's not fair!

Once we finished chai and pakoras, Raghav Guleria started the conversation and never stopped. He took us around the haveli, whose restoration work had been going on for the last few years. It would still take many more, I thought to myself. It's not an easy task. The restoration work is a battle against time itself, a weight that you carry not on your shoulders, but in your soul. Raghav's face told all that story.

"You see these bricks?" his voice interrupted my thoughts. The unfinished wall, a stark reminder of his journey, stood tall in front of us. "These are Nanakshahi bricks. You'd find them in Mughal and Sikh buildings too. I'm trying to capture that same historic beauty, you know, bring the past back to life."

Raghav's eyes lit up every time he spoke of the forgotten artistry hidden in these ruins. Too bad his audience was not well-versed in the subject, but he did not seem to mind that. Like an experienced teacher guiding his new students, he explained every detail with great patience. Across the hall, a large window brought a breath of fresh air. On the other side of it, a shimmering expanse of water stretched out. It was Pong Dam Lake.

"Can you tell me a little about your family connections?" I asked Raghav as we sat next to the fire.

"Sure," he said. "My grandfather was the Raja of Guler. After he passed away, the eldest son took the throne. But tragedy struck again, and he too passed away. That left grandson in line to be the Raja."

"The other grandson, you mean?" I quipped.

"Yes."

"What happened then?" I asked.

"Umm, the grandson wasn't interested in ruling. First, he left Guler, and when he came back, he sold off much of the assets."

"That's a shame."

"Indeed," he said. "Thankfully, my mother had the foresight to buy this place before everything got sold off. So, when my turn came, I knew what I had to do: preserve it for the future."

"How long do you think it will take?"

"I cannot say," he sounded a little sad, as he turned his head away and scrutinised every part of the building. "The government isn't helping much. They do not understand the value of cultural heritage."

"Isn't there anyone who can help?"

"You know, there was a time when our Rajas used to sit next to the viceroy," he smiled. "Sadly those times are behind us."

I kept looking at him. The burden of the past wasn't just in the bricks of the haveli, it was also reflected in Raghav's eyes.

"I want to restore the glory of Guler," Raghav said, just before we bade him goodbye.

"I have no doubt about that."

On my way back to Dharamshala, I thought about a lot of things. Democracies, I wondered, have turned the tables. It has brought freedom for me, by letting me do things my ancestors wouldn't have imagined. But it has also brought trouble for some, by making them do things their ancestors wouldn't have imagined. That's life, I suppose. A constant flow. Good days turn bad, and bad days turn good. The wheel of time keeps turning.

VIII

A Visit to Dari Mela

I have known Aurelie since 2017. Back then, she was travelling in India with Trevor, who is now her husband. Aurelie (or Lili as she is affectionately called) is French, married to a Brit, living in Germany, yet India holds a special place in her heart. The chaos of Indian crowds (which annoys most of us) makes her happy. We, as Indians, do not always appreciate this chaos—and it's understandable. Sometimes outsiders see the magic in our world we take for granted.

Lili, who comes from a neuroscience background and is now a yoga teacher, has made India her second home. Yoga intrigues her, how subtly and intricately it affects every aspect of our mind and body. Once again, I may not share this intrigue, but I can understand it. For some, yoga is a language of the body, a way to speak when words fall short. I, somehow, prefer words even when their meanings stumble, landing me in trouble.

Lili's love for India and Indians is not a one-way street. People here are also fond of her. Don't we always love white people, whatever our reasons may be? I have met so many

Indians who believe that white skin automatically translates to overflowing bank accounts. This belief leads to an occasional 'accidental' bump into a White person followed by a desperate pursuit of friendship. Then there's the 'love guru' school of thought, where a white partner is seen as a passport to a more glamorous life. Also, it's mostly the hippies that travel to the small towns of India—and it's hard not to enjoy their company.

April, 2018:

Lili had come to Dharamshala on a holiday. It wasn't quite spring yet; a hesitant goodbye to the miserly winter was still lingering. Rains lashed the mountains in the first few days of the month, spiced up by the occasional hailstorm that rattled the windows. Thunderstorms are no joke in the mountains. A flash of light explodes in the sky, followed by a BOOM, as if a bomb has exploded nearby. It's scary!

In most of India, the seasons seem to rush from one extreme to the next, leaving this elusive in-between space almost non-existent. But here, in the Himalayas, Dharamshala likes to hold onto a slice of spring. It is the time for rhododendrons to peek through the midget trees. So far... they hadn't shown up.

It was also the time for Mela (local fair) to arrive. This nomadic marketplace wasn't tied to one place, instead, it would travel the gypsy way from Palampur to Nagrota, Joginder Nagar, and Chamunda before finally landing here in Dharamshala. There was also a smaller one in McLeod Ganj, but we had missed it.

"We're not going to miss this one," Lili and I reminded each other.

Despite hearing about the mela quite a few times, neither Lili nor I knew much about its whereabouts. Somebody said it's in Dari. But where was Dari? I did not know at that point. Armed with vague directions, we took a shared cab to Dharamshala. It cost us fifteen rupees per person; these days, it's twenty. It's a pity that the joy of the journey wasn't exactly included in the price. Think of a livestock car crammed with people, all praying for a swift arrival. That's how we spent the next half an hour.

From Dharamshala, Dari was only a quick two-kilometre bus ride further towards Palampur.

As soon as we stepped off the bus, the cacophony of the mela—a clear giveaway of its location surged through the main gate.

The road leading to the mela ground was buzzing with excitement. Long queues snaked along either side. The air shimmered with the aroma of a hundred different street foods—spicy samosas, sizzling pakoras, and jalebis that went round and round, vying for our attention. There were all kinds of sounds. Cars blasted their horns, vendors hawked their toys, and children's cries cut through it all. That's India for you.

"It's such a chaos," I said to Lili.

"That's why I love it," she giggled. "You never know what you are going to get here."

"That's what concerns me..."

Entering Dari Mela Ground, the main venue, felt like travelling back in time. Rusted swings and shaky rides, reminding me of childhood days, stood proudly under the watchful gaze of ancient-looking loudspeakers that blared invitations in broken voices. Lili attracted frequent glances from the stall vendors. Perhaps they wondered what brought a white girl to the mela. The two of us, though, without a worry in our heads, kept browsing.

One thing especially caught our attention. A towering wooden structure loomed ahead, its platform adorned with faded banners proclaiming the legendary "Maut Ka Kuan."

"What's that thing?" Lili did not know about it.

You, too, may not have heard of it. So, let me explain.

Imagine a giant bucket, made of creaky wood instead of plastic. Now, imagine motorcycles and cars roaring around the inside walls, defying gravity as they go up and down at high speeds. That, dear reader, is the not-so-subtle exploit of Maut Ka Kuan, or to say in English "The Well of Death."

The deeper we ventured, the more intriguing the mela got. Lili spotted another great performance on the opposite end of the ground—a local wrestling competition.

We grabbed steaming cups of chai and settled in with the best seats in the house—a small wooden bench with barely enough space for two people. I noticed most people were standing, which made our bench feel like a privilege. Now we turned our attention to the show. There were at least twenty or thirty wrestlers—all with big bellies and slim legs. Each one wore a red langot, a type of loincloth common in Indian wrestling.

The real dose of entertainment came from the commentators. These guys announced the matches with the sincerity of theatre actors, bellowing instructions like, "Next up, we have Sheru the Tiger versus Bunty the Body Builder! Remember boys, a clean fight. No wedgies are allowed in this competition. No touching! No undressing!" Those words had us snorting into our chai.

On our way back, my gaze kept darting to the crowds. All of it used to be just noise and movement, a sensory overload. Not anymore... Somehow in that moment, with eyes a little more open, I saw the symphony beneath the cacophony. Each honking car, each chai stall, each stray dog wandering by—they all seemed to move to their own rhythm.

India isn't a country that reveals itself all at once. It unfolds like a hand-painted scroll, revealing its secrets inch by inch. Most of us get caught in the grandeur of its past or the promises of its future, but India isn't about either. It's about savouring the swirl of life around you, in this moment.

IX

Doctor Sahab's Literary Prescription

Doctor Sahab has spent most of his life in Dharamshala. Originally from Punjab, he moved to the town in his younger years. While he worked as a psychiatrist at the local government hospital, many who knew him saw him more as a cross-disciplinary guru. His appetite for books was insatiable—every spare moment was spent in the company of at least one, if not more. So, when the retirement arrived, he chose to stay in the mountains, surrounded by his beloved books.

Doctor Sahab lives in Indru Nag. Now, where is that?

Have you ever seen those colourful paragliders soaring above Dharamshala? If you can identify their launching spot, that's Indru Nag for you. The place (as you would have got a clue from its name) also houses a temple dedicated to a local snake deity. Hence, the word Nag in it.

Legend has it that a yearly ritual reenacts the battle between gods and demons, and a snake's appearance at the temple the next day predicts the coming season's rain. Such battles are not uncommon in these parts. For example, the Mandi district has a similar tradition where people say that witches fly in to participate in a contest with the gods. As a child, I would frequently hear about women in my neighbourhood who supposedly possessed this ability. What made it scarier was that the women never denied those rumours.

Coming to Indru Nag... how do we get there? From Dharamshala's main market, head towards Khaniyara Road. After about a kilometre or so, from the village of Darnu, take a left turn. Indru Nag awaits you a short distance up the road. For a more scenic route, I recommend the walk up from Darnu itself.

It's a pleasant walk. You might encounter some monkeys along the way, but that's fine, they're usually content to play the watching game as long as you do the same. The path goes through a small village, where you'll see cattle grazing in courtyards and locals going about their day at a leisurely pace. After a 20–30-minute walk, you'll reach Indru Nag. It's a peaceful spot, mostly visited by a handful of devotees and paragliding enthusiasts.

The first time I went there, I felt extremely hungry. Scanning the hilltop for food options, my eyes landed on a solitary cafe hiding among the local houses and shops. I rushed towards the counter where a man was standing, perhaps waiting for a morning customer.

"Do you serve breakfast?" I asked.

"Yes," he responded. "There is paratha, sandwich, maggi noodles..."

"That will do." This was more than I could ask for.

The man told me that he was from the Gaddi tribe, working here for the owner.

"Who is the owner?" I asked.

"Doctor Sahab."

"Doctor Sahab?"

Stepping inside the seating area, I was greeted by a surprising sight—a tiny library tucked away amidst the tables and chairs. Its bookshelves overflowed with a nice mix of volumes, spanning at least a few centuries. A closer look revealed a focus on psychology, religion, and the partition of India and Pakistan. Doctor Sahab must have been a Punjabi interested in the psychological aspect of religion (a deadly combination if you think about it), a guess that became evident moments later when the cafe's owner himself entered the room. A man in his seventies, Doctor Sahab carried a warm smile and a glint of knowledge in his eyes behind the thick spectacles.

"Hello sir," I said.

"Hello," he nodded.

Everything was slow about his demeanour. He was like an old lama, meditating in every step he took. Unlike the hurried rush of young folks chasing the next dopamine hit on their phones, he savoured the slowness of his movements. I could tell that he was mentally collecting the world around him—the warmth of the sun on his face, the gentle chirp of a nearby bird.

"Such a nice library," I said.

"Thank you," he said. "It's an old collection. I thought, maybe someone else could read them too."

"I would love to."

I picked a few of them, mostly partition literature, and started devouring them along with the breakfast. Doctor Sahab sat at the table next to me and had his breakfast at a gentle pace. We exchanged a few words in between. He told me about his life. After his retirement, he decided to stay in Dharamshala instead of going back to his birthplace Amritsar. He set up a guest house and a cafe. What about his family? Did he ever get married? I could not muster the courage to ask such questions.

"It sounds like a different Punjab," I said, closing the book and thinking about it.

"It was," Doctor Sahab responded. "But the world changes..."

"Yes, it's surely not the same," I said. "I mean, people literally used to believe in all sorts of magical creatures just a few generations back."

"That is one way of looking."

"What do you mean?"

"See, it's like this. We, as humans, like to have narratives in our minds. We tell stories. Sometimes we tell the stories of angels and dragons and wizards, and sometimes that of Big-Bang or electrons. In the end, everything is just a story."

"There has to be some ultimate reality, isn't it?"

"That's probably another story, bigger than all of us and beyond our imagination."

"Hmm..." I thought about it throughout the day.

Last winter, when I returned to Indru Nag, the climb felt familiar, but the place itself had changed. New buildings, likely hotels, dotted the landscape. Even Doctor Sahab's cafe looked different. Gone was the cosy charm; it had a sleek, modern feel. This wasn't the old man's style, that much was clear. With a more professional smile, a young man greeted me as I entered.

"Where is Doctor Sahab?" I asked him.

"Oh, he? He does not live here anymore," he said. The young man had a Delhi accent, much different from the old Gaddi fellow. "He moved to a new house recently."

"What about this cafe?"

"We run it now."

"And the library?"

"The books are exactly where they used to be."

I went in. There were those familiar books lining the shelves, along with a brand-new collection. The cafe itself had got an upgrade—more tables, a wider menu, and colourful walls. But something was missing. The air lacked the old, comforting aroma, a mix of dampness and well-worn paperbacks. It felt true what they say—it's the people that make a place special, not the things.

X

The Dog Family

I have said this before: Dharamshala is as much a place for dogs as it is for humans. These friendly creatures seem to have the run of the place. They are everywhere. Look around and you will find them curled up in sunny spots, napping peacefully in the middle of the town chatter. Even local cafes have their own furry angels—mesmerising you with those puppy eyes, literally. And if you're planning a trek to Triund, be prepared for some unexpected companions! These adventurous stray dogs often join trekkers along the way, happy for a scratch behind the ears, and some biscuits, of course.

This story is around the time of the Covid lockdown, in 2020. We were all confined to our homes, working on our laptops, and occasionally, peering out windows with uncertainty—would we see this through? Thankfully, we did... and both you and I made it here.

I was living down in Dharamshala, near that mela place called Dari. If you want me to be more specific, it was on the Darnu-Barol road. I used to be all alone in the house, except that a female dog had adopted me.

Two things to note here: one, I hesitate to use the word *bitch* as I have kept that for more suitable purposes; two, I never adopted her, she did. She started frequenting the house, looking for a chance meal, and eventually, the frequency went up and then she never left.

Did she have a name? Not quite. If anything, I used to call her Dogan.

Dogan was no ordinary dog. She had a husband, or so I liked to believe. Because it seemed like a monogamous relationship. The two would stay together. Even when the lady got pregnant, the husband took care of her, and once the puppies (five of them) arrived, he took care of them as well.

I don't know if you have ever seen a dog family, or a dog society, as the two are not very different. But they are different from a human family. In a dog family, if there is a biscuit on the table, the quickest puppy gets it. It's simple. In a human family, on the other hand, the culture is slightly more complicated. If there is a biscuit on the table, you first invent a game, then you educate all the children about that game, and when the training is over, you ask them to play the game and then the winner of it gets the biscuit as a reward. To make matters culturally appropriate, you ask the winner to be more compassionate and share it with others. None of this happens in a dog family. Certainly not in the one I am discussing here; I cannot comment on what your dogs are up to.

In our story, too, the fastest of these puppies used to get hold of most of the biscuits. He was the shortest of all. I used to call him Dogu, for that specific reason. Dogu was short but he would make up for it by his excessive jumping drills. He would jump to such a height that the other puppies wouldn't be able to get any biscuits. So, to bring some socialism into the dogs' world, I had to grab Dogu while distributing biscuits to his siblings. That worked, on most days.

One morning, surprisingly, I found no puppy or dog outside. Had they been stolen? I was considering all these possibilities when I noticed a movement at one corner of the yard. I ran in that direction. It was Dogu, lying on the ground, sobbing. When I picked him up, his foot appeared to be badly hurt. It was hanging limply at his side. The wound was deep, revealing the tender flesh and pink muscle beneath the torn skin of the paw. Worse, Dogu was now puking, making me worried about his chances of survival.

I called the veterinary centre. Nobody picked. Then I called the dog rescue centre. They were quick to respond.

"Can you help me?" I pleaded.

"What's the matter?" a man from the other side said.

"There is a little puppy that needs your help. He is badly injured."

"Got it. Just tell me your address and we will be there soon."

"Thank you. Just come to the Barol bus stand and let me know."

I kept checking the time, each second stretching into an eternity. My hands wouldn't stop trembling as I held Dogu. Half an hour went by, filled with panicked thoughts of what might happen. Would those people be able to help?

Finally, a distant rumble grew into the unmistakable sound of an approaching jeep. Thank God! The team had arrived. They took the puppy gently, his tiny body resisting as much as it could. My heart ached as they carried him away, but the team member comforted me.

"Don't worry," the driver said to me kindly. "We'll take good care of him here until he's back on his paws."

"Should I come with you?"

"No, it's fine. The COVID protocols don't allow that," he said. "We'll call you once he recovers. Until then, he will be safe with us. Don't worry."

I was relieved. At the same time, I kept hoping and praying that I would see that wagging tail again.

As the day went on, I got busy with chores. There was silence in the house, broken only by the occasional cry from the other puppies. They huddled together, confused and whimpering, the playful energy dampened by a shared anxiety.

Finally, as the sun was about to set, a familiar form emerged in the distance. It was Dogan, I could see through the window. Beside her, walked her husband. They approached cautiously, their ears perked and noses twitching. The puppies shouted, jumping around them in anxiety. But Dogan remained still, her gaze fixed on the empty space on the mat where her puppy once lay.

I could feel the helplessness in my room. Language, our main tool of communication, now felt utterly useless. How could I explain the sequence of events? Words seemed insignificant compared to the pain on Dogan's face as she nosed at the ground, her frantic licks searching for a familiar scent that was no longer there.

"She could assume that I have harmed her child," I thought to myself.

Thankfully, she did not. The minute I opened the door and went outside, she came to me and started licking. There was no aggression, no growl to accompany the sharp barks that erupted from her throat. Instead, a heartbreaking whine trembled through the air, a sound that spoke of a mother's deep anguish. I could feel a lump in my throat. If only I could bridge the language barrier, explain what happened in the day, the assurances, the promise of Dogu's return, and more. I wish that could happen. In reality... faced with those mournful cries, being human felt utterly inadequate.

XI

A Trek to Triund

Go on a trek to Triund. That's what they advertise all the time, don't they? Lush green meadows sprawling endlessly, majestic snow-capped Dhauladhars in the background, a perfect setting for an Instagram photo. Still, I believe, those advertisements don't do justice to the place. The way your heart soars after the final climb; your lungs might burn but a smile stretches wide across your face. You have to try it once.

The year was 2012. I had traded the scorching Delhi summer for a refreshing breath of crisp Dharamshala air. The next morning, I set off for Triund. As customary here, a stray dog who'd decided I was worthy of companionship, walked happily beside me. The morning felt cool and quiet, and the only sounds were the rhythmic crunch of my boots and the melodic chirping of unseen birds.

As I was about to hum a song, a strange voice filled the air, singing another song. *Pardesi pardesi jana nahin...* (Perhaps a touch too sentimental for a trek, I conceded with a chuckle.) A few more steps and... I came face-to-face with a young couple, their faces red with exertion.

"Looks like we all love Bollywood songs here," I said, smiling.

"Yes," the woman replied and introduced herself. "Hello, I am Pema."

"Deepak."

"JK."

"That's an interesting name," I said as I sat next to them under a small tree.

"The full name is just a mouthful, so I stick with JK."

"Ha-ha. So how did you learn this Hindi song?"

"I taught him," Pema said proudly as she got up. "Let's keep going."

Despite questionable singing voices, we continued to sing and walk, ever upwards. Whenever they struggled with lyrics, I helped them. I have this awkward tendency to become the lyrics police on occasion, in the hope of protecting the sanctity of every word. I know it's annoying, but I keep failing to recover from this condition.

Pema and JK did not mind it, thankfully. As we trekked, they entertained me with tales of their travels in India. Unlike what I had initially thought, they were not a couple. JK, all the way from Taiwan, had come to learn about the Dalai Lama's home, and Pema was his local guide. We reached the Magic View Cafe, which was aptly named, I thought. Looking down, we could see Dharamshala sprawled out like a colourful carpet, houses clinging to the hillside. There was a feeling of calm here. Across the valley, fluffy sheep and stubborn goats grazed, their occasional bleats created therapeutic sounds.

The final stretch was a killer—our legs screamed with every step. But we kept going, and wow, was the struggle worth it? The view was unreal. The Dhauladhars stretched out before us, a jaw-dropping panorama of snow-capped peaks reaching for the sky. We couldn't help ourselves—we erupted in victory cheers and jumped around, drawing curious glances from other trekkers. It did not matter; nothing matters when you're at the top of the world. Finally, we collapsed onto the soft grass, breathing hard but still laughing like fools. The feeling of accomplishment, the fresh air, the incredible scenery—it was pure joy.

"We have to go back," Pema said to me, about fifteen minutes after we'd reached there.

"So early?"

"Yes, JK has to catch a bus tonight."

"What's the time right now?"

"It's almost three o'clock."

"What? Where did the time go?" I wondered and immediately realised that it was the tragedy of the good times. They arrive too late and leave too early.

"Let's have some chai at least," I insisted.

That's what we did next. The tea seller poured steaming cups of chai as we sat huddled together. Pema and JK emptied their cups within no time, whereas I took my own sweet time.

"We should leave now," Pema said, gathering all her stuff.

"See you around," we said to each other. The traveller's goodbye is a well-worn phrase, a promise exchanged countless times but rarely fulfilled. *But you never know...* That's what we say to ourselves when we say "See you" to fellow travellers. With such lingering thoughts, I waved goodbye to them. The warmth of the teacup seeped into my hands as I watched their figures shrink until they disappeared in the distance.

Soon the day ended without me realising it. Alone now, I unfurled my sleeping bag and gazed into the sky. It was something to behold. Millions of stars twinkled down, a celestial wonder, unlike anything I'd ever seen. I lay transfixed under the stars, but my mind wandered in all directions. Big questions, like the universe's secrets or life's meaning, swirled alongside the smaller ones, like how did my day go? My own life felt tangled in comparison to Pema and JK's easy joy. I wished I could be happy like them. As the cold air settled, I drifted off to sleep, the stars keeping a silent watch.

After spending a couple of nights in Triund, I descended back to McLeod Ganj. As I wandered through the narrow streets, looking for a comfortable space to sit and have some food, a familiar face caught my eye. Pema! I had to look twice to be sure. She was sitting outside a café on the Temple Road.

"Pema? I don't believe this!" I said, surprised.

"Hey!" She looked up, a sense of recognition lighting up her eyes. "Deepak? How nice to see you again."

There we were... The traveller's promise of seeing each other again had been fulfilled.

"What are you reading?" I asked, noticing a book clutched in her hands.

"I, uh," she stammered, her cheeks flushing a light pink. "I am trying to learn English."

"I don't think you need to."

"I don't know about that. Anyway," she pulled a chair. "Why don't you join me? I will get to practise some English."

"You already speak such good English."

"Don't flatter me," she smiled. "Let me get some chai for you. I know you like it."

"I love it."

We sat side-by-side and had chai. We talked for a while, about this and that—and as conversations sometimes do, ours drifted deeper. That's when she shared her personal journey. Her voice, though soft, held a quiet strength as she spoke of her husband who had abandoned her in Arunachal Pradesh, leaving her with two young children. Hoping for better employment opportunities, she moved here to live with her sister.

Pema's life wasn't as rosy as I'd imagined on the trek. "Life is tough," she said, "especially for women." There were many like her, she added, women who had crossed treacherous borders, clinging to the dream of a better life.

"Why Dharamashala?" I asked. "You can get better opportunities in big cities."

"His Holiness," she answered in an instant. There was a spark of hope in her eyes when she mentioned the Dalai Lama. That's what faith does, I *believe.*

"It's not easy," Pema said after a few moments of silence. "But we are strong. We have to be, for our children."

"You are strong, Pema," I reassured her. "I am sure life will get better now."

"I wish I could do nothing," she said, "and make a lot of money."

"Ha-ha. That won't happen," I said, wondering if she was that silly. "You have to work for it, right?"

"I am not sure…"

That was more than ten years ago. These days, she makes TikTok videos and earns far more than I have ever done. Look who's silly now!

XII

A Childhood Memory Revisited

I was 10. My father had just been transferred to a faraway land called Kaza (that's what happens when you fail to please the politicians), which meant, my summer holidays were going to be spent there. The journey from Palampur to Kaza was a long one, three days to be precise. (We travelled during the day and rested at night).

It went something like this: Day 1 at Shimla, Day 2 at Reckong Peo, and at the end of Day 3, there it was—Kaza.

Kaza was a cold desert, yet, considering the absence of civilisation in most parts of Spiti Valley, it was nothing less than a hotspot.

On one side, there ran the Spiti river—roaring and rumbling, without realising the fact that it would soon lose its identity to Sutlej. On the other side, people said, you would find Tibetan villages if you keep travelling for a day or two, and eventually, Chinese soldiers would detain you! I never tried that option.

The town sat at an altitude of 12,000 feet. There were few trees—only as many as I could count at that time. I did not understand what it meant, until, I dashed down the stairs and sprinted towards the river, and my nose started to bleed. Kitty, my elder sister, explained the science of low oxygen and atmospheric pressure. I did not listen, but only stared at the blood and cried.

The real vacation began the next day onwards, when we started to play cricket. There was a huge ground, right next to the house: we never saw the end of it, nor did we try to walk that far. I loved the sight of it. But, at the same time, the vastness of this ground confused us. Until then, we had only played on the terraced fields of our hills, and therefore, we used to hit the ball on one side of the wicket. But here? Here, we could hit anywhere, and as far as possible. It was a big deal!

We talked about it for hours.

And then arrived this guy: a typical Spiti boy, with dry, rosy cheeks. He appeared two to three years older and smelled of sheep that he was shepherding. He said something, which we did not understand. Then we asked him his name etc, which he did not understand. This is not too uncommon; almost every district speaks in a different tongue in our state. Somehow, after a few verbal and non-verbal exchanges, we were able to figure out that he wanted to play cricket. And so began a quiet friendship.

Every day, he would wait outside our house, and call me—not by name, of course. He would yell in his own tongue, whistle or simply howl. Then I would bring the kit and the two of us would play. I batted and he bowled, most of the time; and when he batted, I signalled him not to hit the ball too far, and he complied. He never complained. We did not exchange any words, only sometimes, when I said something and he said something in reply and we laughed at the circumstances. I wanted to ask him about a lot of things. What was his name? Where was his family? Why didn't he go to school? Did he consider me a friend? Unfortunately, it never happened.

Then, one day, I left, not to be returned for many years. When I said goodbye—which was the day before I left—I could not convey that I was going back home. He thought it was a normal goodbye and ran towards his sheep. The next morning, when I sat on a bus, I thought of him. That he would be waiting outside the house. Perhaps whistling! Would he be upset too? That we would never meet again? The bus played a Kishore Kumar song. *Akela gaya tha main, na aya akela, mere sang sang aya teri yaadon ka mela.*

XIII

A Himachali Folktale

As we come to the final few pages, let me share a local legend that has been passed down through generations.

Now, if you know anything about Himachal, or its neighbouring regions along the Himalayas, such as Uttarakhand, Ladakh or Nepal, you would know that people lead a simple here. It's not surprising. When you are struggling to survive in high altitudes, battling all kinds of wild animals, demons or ghosts, you are going to focus a lot more on doing the basics right. This has been the theme throughout history in these parts.

Therefore, when there was no democracy and kingdoms—really small ones, to be fair—flourished, even the kings and queens could not afford a lavish lifestyle. In fact, when you read about their lifestyles, you are going to pity them and be grateful that you are a common folk of the twenty-first century and not among the royalty of *that* era.

This folk story is about one such king. Raja Bana Bhat, as he was called. He used to earn his living by making ropes and selling them at a fair price. Hence the name, Bana. His wife, the queen, was called Mehto. And she too, did not live anything like a queen. She did all the household chores and drew water in an earthen pot from a well near the fort early in the morning. The days were busy too. She used to spin as both she and the king wore handspun cloth only. So much for the royalty...

The kingdom was not a socialist one, it was more like what capitalists keep dreaming about but never achieve. People did not pay taxes, and yet, they had plenty to eat, thanks to the humility (some might use the word *stupidity*) of its rulers. Overall things were going pretty well. So, where is the plot twist? It's coming, wait for it.

Once a big fair was being held in Kangra. People from all age groups came to see it and went shopping.

The king and the queen were also there. But unlike most people, who had put on the flashiest clothes for the occasion, these two were in their usual dress. They moved among the crowd freely. No security guards, protocols, etc. Why would there be? It's not like the royal couple was filthy rich. Some of the merchants were richer than them.

One of these merchants' wives was wearing a necklace worth nine lakhs of rupees (navlakha). When the queen saw her, she felt jealous. It's either human nature or women have been mistakenly portrayed this way in stories—I can't say. But, coming to our story, the queen felt that she too must possess one such necklace. Look at the humility, though. She wasn't trying to get ahead of that woman, she was only seeking equality.

Mehto, the queen, did not give up on her demand, and eventually, the king had to find a way to get her the necklace. How would he do that? "I have an idea," he thought. "Let me tax my subjects and that is that."

What followed next was exactly what the right-wing Americans have been screaming all along.

SOCIAL WELFARE MAKES YOU LAZY. IT MAKES YOU POOR. GODDAMNIT!

So the next time when the king got sick and he asked the queen for some water, she could not fetch any. When she tied its neck (pot's not king's) with a rope, she could not lift it from the well and dropped it. She had lost her ability to work. Since there were no servants now, thanks to welfare schemes, and feminism was still a few centuries away, the king could not get water and passed away. The queen wept and wept and died a few days later.

That day the people of Himachal decided that they would focus more on making ropes and less on necklaces. So far, so good!

Afterword

Maybe you're a visitor, just beginning your exploration of Dharamshala. If that's the case, breathe in the cool mountain air, and let the tranquillity of the Himalayas settle over you. As you navigate the winding streets and colourful monasteries, remember, the true essence of this place lies in its people. Strike up a conversation with a chai wallah, share a smile with a Tibetan on their morning walk, and listen to their stories. You'll be surprised by the wisdom and warmth.

Or maybe, Dharamshala has become your home, a place you return to for solace or a deeper connection. And if that's the case, I may have some questions for you, dear reader. Have you noticed something worth sharing that I may have missed here?

This is where our conversation continues. If a story resonated with you, if your own experience in Dharamshala sparked a reflection you'd like to share, I'd love to hear from you.

Dharamshala's magic lies not just in its landscape, but in the stories of human experiences woven within it. Share yours with me, and together, we can keep the stories of this special place alive.

You can reach me at the following email address: authordeepakrana@gmail.com

Until next time, may your journey in Dharamshala be filled with peace, connection, and a deeper understanding of yourself.

www.ingramcontent.com/pod-product-compliance
Lightning Source LLC
Chambersburg PA
CBHW031453150726
47990CB00007B/2733